JESUS
PROM

STUDY GUIDE

JESUS PROM

Life Gets Fun
When You Love People
Like God Does

JON WEECE
with Dixon Kinser

NELSON
BOOKS

An Imprint of Thomas Nelson

Published in Nashville, Tennessee, by Nelson Books, an imprint of Thomas Nelson. Nelson Books and Thomas Nelson are registered trademarks of HarperCollins Christian Publishing, Inc.

Thomas Nelson titles may be purchased in bulk for educational, business, fund-raising, or sales promotional use. For information, please e-mail SpecialMarkets@ ThomasNelson.com.

All Scripture quotations are taken from The Holy Bible, *New International Version*®, *NIV*®. Copyright © 1973, 1978, 1984, 2011 by Biblica, Inc.® Used by permission. All rights reserved worldwide.

ISBN 978-0-5291-1168-5

First Printing August 2014 / Printed in the United States of America

contents

introduction

If you live in the United States, one of the questions you're likely to hear at a dinner party is, "Where do you go to church?" Going to church has been part of American culture for a long time—especially in the South. In fact, people sometimes use it as shorthand to describe their association with organized Christianity. "I go to church" or "I don't go to church" are ways of explaining whether or not a person is into faith, because the assumption is that church is a place where people go.

However, the phrase "going to church" is actually a misnomer. No one can "go to church" because the church is not a *place*. The church is people. The New Testament talks about the church as the people of God. That means the church is not a place where we go but instead is a kind of community we are. The church has its character because it does things, and what the church does speaks to what it is.

This definition begs another question: What kind of things do our churches do? When we act in our world, are we doing things that God cares about? Are we joining God in putting the broken things back together? Are we making our public life look like God looks? Or are we up to other things?

These are the questions that drive *Jesus Prom*. For the next six sessions, we will be exploring a half dozen different verbs. These are the verbs that define what the people of God — or the church — are invited to be doing in the world. Those six verbs — *love*, *be*, *see*, *dance*, *give*, and *remember* — are not ideas but invitations. They are a direction for being the church in the world. As such, this study is not going to be primarily about ideas but about action.

Each session will explore a different aspect of the verbs of God through the teachings and stories of Jon Weece. There will be an opening question, a little Bible study, and then you'll watch Jon on video. However, the real action comes after the video is over, when you dig into each topic in a guided small-group time. During that portion of the study, your group will be invited into a practical experiment designed to put that session's verb into practice. This section, called "Being the Church," should serve as a place where the big ideas of *Jesus Prom* take on a flesh-and-blood reality.

It's going to be great. Really. However, if want to get the most out of your *Jesus Prom* experience, keep a couple of things in mind. First, the real growth in this study will happen during your small-group time. This is where you will process the content of Jon's message, ask questions, and learn from others as you listen to what God's love is doing in their lives.

This leads to point two. Small groups can be a deeply rewarding time of intimacy and friendship, but they can also be a disaster. So work to make your group a "safe place." That means being honest about your thoughts and feelings as well as listening carefully to everyone else's opinions.

Third, resist the temptation to "fix" a problem that someone might be having or to correct someone's theology. That's not what this time is for. In addition, keep everything that your group shares confidential. All this will foster a rewarding sense of community in your *Jesus Prom* group and give God's Spirit some space to heal, challenge, and send you out to *do* the verbs that show our world the love of God.

One last thing.

You might have wondered why this study is called *Jesus Prom*. The name comes from a party that Jon's church throws every year for the disabled, handicapped, and mentally ill. It's a beautiful thing, and Jon speaks about it in session 4 of the study and chapter 9 of the book. "Jesus Prom" is something Jon's community came up with to be the church in their neighborhood—something they devised and created. This study is designed to help *you* figure out how to be creative in the same way. How can you be the church in your neighborhood? What is your "Jesus Prom"? That's the question you should be asking as you move through the sessions.

So experiment, dream, and risk, but whatever you do, please don't do nothing. As Jon says, the call of God

is for the church to love the verbs that God loves.
So get out there, jump in with both feet, and take
these words — *love, be, see, dance, give, remember* —
and make them flesh!

how to use this guide

As you'll discover throughout this study, *Jesus Prom* is very practical. It gets out there and does things. It takes risks. Jon found out that his life got fun when he loved people like God does, so this study is designed to give you similar opportunities.

Each session in *Jesus Prom* begins with a mixer question followed by a reflection from the Bible. You will then watch a video clip and jump into some directed small-group discussion. Even though multiple questions are provided, don't feel that you have to use them all. Your leader will focus on the ones that resonate with your group and guide you from there.

The final component of each session—called "Being the Church"—is where this study might diverge from others you have done in the past. During this time, you and your group will engage in a hands-on exercise that puts the verb featured during the session into practice. These exercises are meant to be completed during your meeting and will be what you make of them. If you choose to only go through the motions, or if you abstain from participating in these exercises, there is less chance you'll find what you're looking for during this time. However, if you stay open and take a gamble, you may discover what so many others have already found to be true: your faith will come alive when you take holy risks for God!

Now, the thought of "risky" activities might make some folks feel anxious. That's okay. If you fall into this category, then just read ahead to each "Being the Church" section, and you will know what's coming up. Then you can prepare yourself accordingly. Remember, none of these experiments involves anything inappropriate or embarrassing. They are just hands-on opportunities to train in loving like God loves.

At the end of each session, there are three more opportunities for you to engage the content of *Jesus Prom* during the coming week. Jon says that love is "a profound affection, put into action," so each part of this section is a variation on that theme. The first is activity-based ("Affection in Action"), the second is a biblical reflection ("Affection in Devotion"), and the third is a meditation based on a chapter from the book ("Affection in Instruction"). The challenge will be to do at least one of these activities between sessions and to use your study guide to record what you learn.

Starting in session 2, you will be given time before the video to check in with your group about the previous week's activity and process your experiences. If you could not do an activity one week, or if you are just joining the study, don't worry. Hearing what others have learned will be nourishment enough.

Finally, remember that this is an opportunity to train yourself in a new way of seeing the world. The videos, discussions, and activities are simply meant to kick-start your imagination so that you start coming up with ideas and trying new things on your own. After all, what do you think God could do with a whole group of people who were passionate about Jesus' love and eager to put it into action? Let's jump into *Jesus Prom* and find out.

If you are a group leader, additional instructions and resources for leading the "Being the Church" sections are located in the back of this book. Because some of the activities require materials and setup, make sure you read this section so you will be prepared for each week's activity.

SESSION ONE

love

love (v.) — a profound affection put into action

introduction

Have you ever had one of those emails sitting in your inbox that you just keep putting off? Do you know the one I mean? Chances are it involves something that makes you tired, addresses a conflict, or is basically just going to drain energy from you. And so you wait. Sometimes for weeks. Because when it comes to engaging with draining and difficult relationships, it is not easy put yourself out there.

However, when you read about the life and ministry of Jesus, a strange pattern emerges. Quite unlike that email in our inbox, Jesus seems to move toward the "unfun" and difficult people. Time and again we see him honing in on and making a beeline for the hardest folks to get along with. These are not only some of the most difficult people of his day, but they also include the very folks who end up putting him to death. Why is this? Is Jesus' intent to set some impossible standard that his followers can never hope to achieve? Not even remotely. Jesus is simply doing what he said he would do: showing us what God is really like.

For almost two thousand years, the witness of the church has been that Jesus is the full, total, and complete image of God. What God is like is what Jesus is like, and what Jesus is like is what God is like. This means that it is in the deepest parts of God's nature to move toward challenging and unlovable people, not away from them. For God, there is never a lingering message in the inbox. He is always ready to reply and hit send.

All this begs the question: What about us? How do we deal with the problematic and unlovable people in our lives? Do we wait for them to come to us to have a relationship, or do we, like our God, go to them? When we love others like this, how might it change them? Or how might it change *us*? Furthermore, who are the hardest people for us to love, and what does it mean that God loves them anyway?

These are the questions that we will address in session 1.

welcome and checking in

Go around the group to introduce yourselves and then complete the following sentences:

> One thing you can tell about me from the shoes I'm wearing is _____.

> If I could describe my expectations for this study in one word, that word would be _____.

> The reason that word captures my expectations is because _____
>
> _____.

hearing the word

Read John 4:1–30 (see next page) aloud in the group, listening for a fresh insight during the reading.

¹Now Jesus learned that the Pharisees had heard that he was gaining and baptizing more disciples than John — ²although in fact it was not Jesus who baptized, but his disciples. ³So he left Judea and went back once more to Galilee.

⁴Now he had to go through Samaria. ⁵So he came to a town in Samaria called Sychar, near the plot of ground Jacob had given to his son Joseph. ⁶Jacob's well was there, and Jesus, tired as he was from the journey, sat down by the well. It was about noon.

⁷When a Samaritan woman came to draw water, Jesus said to her, "Will you give me a drink?" ⁸(His disciples had gone into the town to buy food.)

⁹The Samaritan woman said to him, "You are a Jew and I am a Samaritan woman. How can you ask me for a drink?" (For Jews do not associate with Samaritans.)

¹⁰Jesus answered her, "If you knew the gift of God and who it is that asks you for a drink, you would have asked him and he would have given you living water."

¹¹"Sir," the woman said, "you have nothing to draw with and the well is deep. Where can you get this living water? ¹²Are you greater than our father Jacob, who gave us the well and drank from it himself, as did also his sons and his livestock?"

¹³Jesus answered, "Everyone who drinks this water will be thirsty again, ¹⁴but whoever drinks the water I give them will never thirst. Indeed, the water I give them will become in them a spring of water welling up to eternal life."

¹⁵The woman said to him, "Sir, give me this water so that I won't get thirsty and have to keep coming here to draw water."

¹⁶He told her, "Go, call your husband and come back."

¹⁷"I have no husband," she replied.

Jesus said to her, "You are right when you say you have no husband. [18]The fact is, you have had five husbands, and the man you now have is not your husband. What you have just said is quite true."

[19]"Sir," the woman said, "I can see that you are a prophet. [20]Our ancestors worshiped on this mountain, but you Jews claim that the place where we must worship is in Jerusalem."

[21]"Woman," Jesus replied, "believe me, a time is coming when you will worship the Father neither on this mountain nor in Jerusalem. [22]You Samaritans worship what you do not know; we worship what we do know, for salvation is from the Jews. [23]Yet a time is coming and has now come when the true worshipers will worship the Father in the Spirit and in truth, for they are the kind of worshipers the Father seeks. [24]God is spirit, and his worshipers must worship in the Spirit and in truth."

[25]The woman said, "I know that Messiah" (called Christ) "is coming. When he comes, he will explain everything to us."

[26]Then Jesus declared, "I, the one speaking to you— I am he."

[27]Just then his disciples returned and were surprised to find him talking with a woman. But no one asked, "What do you want?" or "Why are you talking with her?"

[28]Then, leaving her water jar, the woman went back to the town and said to the people, [29]"Come, see a man who told me everything I ever did. Could this be the Messiah?" [30]They came out of the town and made their way toward him.

Now turn to the person next to you and take turns sharing:

What was one thing that stood out to you from the reading?

In what way was this a new insight?

What would you say is the point of a story like this?

watch the video

Watch the session 1 video clip, using the space below to take notes. When the video ends, take a moment to reflect and jot down one or two things you learned, disagreed with, or were surprised by.

group discussion

1. Before everyone shares in the group, turn to one or two people next to you and finish this sentence: "After watching the video, one question I now have is …"

2. In the video, Jon emphasizes that Jesus "*had* to go to Samaria." What does it mean to you that Jesus *had* to go there?

3. Jon says that the most difficult people to love are often the ones who don't understand love. Do you think this is true? In your opinion, what makes someone truly difficult to love?

4. Jon tells a story about his church serving a buffet lunch to the patrons and dancers of a local strip club. Was this story interesting, challenging, or offensive to you, and why?

5. Do you think that the ministry in the strip club is valuable only if people there come to Jon's church? Why or why not?

6. What does Deanna's story have to say about God's love?

7. How would your church respond if someone like Deanna was part of your community?

being the church

For this activity, each person will need a pen and an index card.

————

Write down on the card the name of someone in your life who is or has been difficult to love. It can be a current relationship or from any point in your past. It can even be you! If confidentiality is a concern, just write down the initials of the person or some other symbol to denote who the person is.

After everyone has completed the exercise, reflect together on what makes your difficult persons hard to love.

Finally, reflect together on what this difficulty might say about you and the attitude of your hearts.

closing prayer

Close the meeting by praying silently together for a couple of minutes. First, offer a one-word prayer (just one!) for the individual on your card. Next, pray that the person on your left would be able to *give* love to all the people in his or her life who are difficult to love. Finally, pray that the person on your right would be able to *receive* love in healthy ways from God and others.

between-sessions
PERSONAL STUDY AND REFLECTION

You are invited to further explore the challenge of *Jesus Prom* by engaging in any or all of the following between-sessions activities. Remember that this part of *Jesus Prom* is not about following rules or doing your homework — these activities (categorized as "Affection in Action," "Affection in Devotion," and "Affection in Instruction") are simply to give you the opportunity to put this session's verb into practice. *Be sure to read the reflection questions after completing an activity and make a few notes in your study guide about the experience.* There will be a time to share these reflections at the beginning of the next session.

AFFECTION IN ACTION: clean it up!

During the video this week, Jon compares our hearts to the attic of a house crammed full of stuff. He uses the example of people who compulsively hoard things in their homes and notes that their houses did not become full of junk overnight. It takes years to accumulate that much stuff! In the same way, we pick up little hurts, grievances, and offenses during our lives which — if we do not pay attention — can slowly fill the entirety of our hearts so there is little room left for love.

Based on this observation, this week find one project, room, or space in your house that you've been putting off organizing. It could be as small as a bookshelf or as large as your whole garage. As an act of active prayer, clean out that space; and as you are cleaning, meditate on the clutter you may have collected in your heart. What would it look like for God to begin to clean it out? How can you cooperate with him?

Mull this over across the entirety of the project and write down any observations in the journal space below to share next time.

Pray. Clean. God is near.

AFFECTION IN DEVOTION: **be perfect?**

For this week's "Affection in Devotion," read Matthew 5:43 – 48. This passage is from Jesus' Sermon on the Mount, where Jesus describes what love looks like when it's lived out God's way.

> 43"You have heard that it was said, 'Love your neighbor and hate your enemy.' 44But I tell you, love

your enemies and pray for those who persecute you, [45]that you may be children of your Father in heaven. He causes his sun to rise on the evil and the good, and sends rain on the righteous and the unrighteous. [46]If you love those who love you, what reward will you get? Are not even the tax collectors doing that? [47]And if you greet only your own people, what are you doing more than others? Do not even pagans do that? [48]Be perfect, therefore, as your heavenly Father is perfect."

Ironically, from this passage we see that Jesus had to spend some of his time clearing up misunderstandings, especially among his own people. The phrase, "You have heard it said ... but I say," indicates just one of these moral course corrections. In the case above, however, Jesus was not reorienting the way people act, but reorienting the way they love.

Jesus started the teaching by invoking one of the more famous sections of the Old Testament law. In Leviticus 19:18, God instructed his people to love their neighbors as themselves, and while this seems fairly straightforward, by Jesus' day it was not. Over time, the many debates over who exactly counted as a "neighbor" had made the definition of this term grow smaller and smaller. Sure, a neighbor certainly included those who were part of God's people. But what about Israel's enemies? What about the Samaritans, whom they believed were mocking God's laws? Did God really require them to love those people?

That is where the people drew the line. There was an in-group and an out-group, and their enemies fell into the out-group. Their love could stop here. This is what

makes Jesus' redirect of conventional wisdom so radical.
He challenged the people to expand their definition of
"neighbor" to *include* even their enemies. In instructing
the people to love their enemies and pray for those who
persecuted them, he called his followers to be … well,
like God. God, as Jesus explains, shows favor to everyone
regardless of their standing with him. The righteous and
the wicked alike get rain and sun from God, not because
they deserve it but because God loves them. God's love
shows no partiality, so neither should they. For Jesus, love
never drew the line.

- If you could describe your reaction to Jesus'
  teaching in one word, what would that word be?
  _____

- Do you love as God does? Why or why not?

- Whom is it easy to love without conditions? Why?

- Whom is it hard to love without conditions? Why?

- Do you ever put conditions on the way you receive love? If so, what conditions?

- What is one concrete thing you could do this week to expand the boundaries of how you love?

AFFECTION IN INSTRUCTION: jump

Read chapters 1 and 2 of the book *Jesus Prom*, and then answer the following questions.

- Do you find risk to be something exciting or threatening? Explain.

- In chapter 1, Jon offers a list of verbs to bring into your life: *love*, *be*, *see*, *talk*, *rest*, *turn*, *dance*, *give*, *go*, *remember*, *receive*, *die*, and *suffer*. Which of these verbs seems the most appealing to add to your life? Which seems the most challenging? Why did you answer as you did?

- Jon states, "It may seem safe to stand on the deck with the rest of the people. But standing on decks is not safe. It's boring. So go for it. Jump. Set down whatever you are holding onto or whatever has a hold of you and jump." What keeps you from jumping? Is it something you are holding onto or something that's holding you down? How can you get free?

Use the space below to write any key points or questions you want to bring to the next group meeting.

be

be (v.) — to have identity; to equal in meaning

introduction

Have you ever heard someone describe himself or herself as a glass-half-full or glass-half-empty kind of person? It's shorthand for a person's attitude toward his or her circumstances. Are things generally positive (half full) or negative (half empty)?

This same metric is in play with how we view ourselves. If things are going well, our lives feel half full. Conversely, when times are tough and we have experienced failure or loss, it can be easy to see ourselves as half empty. However, this is not how God sees things at all. Sure, we are all broken people in need of a Savior, and in that sense you might say we are all half empty. But when God looks at us, he doesn't focus on our sin and shame. Instead, he sees us as we were meant to be. God sees us as half full.

All of this begs the question of how you see yourself. When you look at your life, are you distracted and overwhelmed by your mistakes and regrets? If so, there's good news for you. This is not how God sees you at all—and furthermore, this is not how God wants you to see yourself. God doesn't first see what's lacking; he sees what he loves. The invitation in this session is to do the same. It is an invitation to see your neighbors and yourself as God does: half full.

Will you take him up on this invitation?

checking in

Go around the group and answer the following question:

Do you tend to drive a clean car or dirty car? (Use a scale of 1 to 10, with 1 being "spotless" and 10 being "a disaster," to rank your vehicle's cleanness. If you do not have a car, use your room, purse, workspace, or locker at school.)

Last week, you were invited to act in the "Between-Sessions Personal Study and Reflection" section. Discuss the following:

- Did you do at least one of the activities? If so, which one? If not, why not?

- What are some of the things you wrote down in reflection?

- What did you learn by engaging in these activities?

- What did you learn about yourself this week? About God?

hearing the word

Read John 3:1–17 aloud in the group, listening for a fresh insight during the reading. Then together discuss the questions that follow.

¹Now there was a Pharisee, a man named Nicodemus who was a member of the Jewish ruling council. ²He came to Jesus at night and said, "Rabbi, we know that you are a teacher who has come from God. For no one could perform the signs you are doing if God were not with him."

³Jesus replied, "Very truly I tell you, no one can see the kingdom of God unless they are born again."

⁴"How can someone be born when they are old?" Nicodemus asked. "Surely they cannot enter a second time into their mother's womb to be born!"

⁵Jesus answered, "Very truly I tell you, no one can enter the kingdom of God unless they are born of water and the Spirit. ⁶Flesh gives birth to flesh, but the Spirit gives birth to spirit. ⁷You should not be surprised at my saying, 'You must be born again.' ⁸The wind blows wherever it pleases. You hear its sound, but you cannot tell where it comes from or where it is going. So it is with everyone born of the Spirit."

⁹"How can this be?" Nicodemus asked.

¹⁰"You are Israel's teacher," said Jesus, "and do you not understand these things? ¹¹Very truly I tell you, we speak of what we know, and we testify to what we have seen, but still you people do not accept our testimony. ¹²I have spoken to you of earthly things and you do not believe; how then will you believe if I speak of heavenly things? ¹³No one has ever gone into heaven except the one who came from heaven—the

Son of Man. ¹⁴Just as Moses lifted up the snake in the wilderness, so the Son of Man must be lifted up ¹⁵that everyone who believes may have eternal life in him."

¹⁶For God so loved the world that he gave his one and only Son, that whoever believes in him shall not perish but have eternal life. ¹⁷For God did not send his Son into the world to condemn the world, but to save the world through him.

When you hear the phrase "born again," what does it make you think of?

What do you think it means to be "born of the Spirit" (v. 8)?

Verse 17 says God is saving the world through Jesus. If this is God's job, what do you think our job is and how is it related to God's job?

watch the video

Watch the session 2 video clip, using the space below to take notes. When the video ends, take a moment to reflect and jot down one or two things you learned, disagreed with, or were surprised by.

group discussion

1. Before everyone shares in the group, turn to one or two people next to you and finish this sentence: "After watching the video, one question I now have is ..."

2. Jon begins the video with this quote from Dostoevsky: "To love a person is to see them as God intended them to be." Do you think this is true? Why or why not?

3. Where in the world today do you see the outside of someone's life lining up or not lining up with the inside of his or her life? How does this make you feel?

4. Jon points out three vignettes from Nicodemus's life, as recorded in the gospel of John, which show a progression of his faith. When we first meet Nicodemus, he is coming to Jesus "at night"; later, he is standing up for Jesus; finally, he is with Jesus all the way to the end. Which one of these stages of Nicodemus's faith describes how you feel this week?

5. What was your impression of the Maas family?

6. How is the Maas family like a picture of what the church is meant to be?

7. Jon says, "We live in a culture where who we are is defined by what we do. Jesus came ... so that what we do is defined by who we are." Do you think this is true? Does it sound like good news? Why or why not?

8. Is it hard or easy for you to believe that when God looks at you, he doesn't see all the junk in your life but instead sees you as you were intended to be? Why did you answer as you did?

being the church

For this activity, each person will need a sheet of lined notebook paper, a sheet of colored construction paper, a pen, scissors, and a glue stick.

———

Jon notes that when Jesus told Nicodemus he could be "born again," it was like an invitation from Jesus to hit the reset button. It was a chance to start over, to begin again. That is exactly what Jesus invites us to do today.

Use the sheet of notebook paper to write down (as neatly as possible) a circumstance in your life for which you would like to hit the reset button. Write at least three sentences to describe this circumstance, including what, in your estimation, caused the problem. You won't be asked to share this—no one will see it but you.

Once you have written about this situation, use the scissors to cut the sentences into individual words. Then rearrange some, or all, of those words to form a prayer and glue it onto the piece of colored construction paper. The prayer should reflect what you want God to redeem, restore, or renew from this circumstance. It's okay if it's short — sometimes the best prayer is just, "Help me!"

closing prayer

Once everyone is finished, gather again as a group and close the session by going around the room and offering your written prayer. If you do not feel comfortable sharing your prayer, just say, "Help me!" God knows what you mean!

Take your prayer home and put it somewhere where you will be reminded to pray it throughout the week. Through this prayer, you are not asking God to change your past but entrusting your past to him, the One who is fully trustworthy and can redeem all things.

between-sessions

PERSONAL STUDY AND REFLECTION

AFFECTION IN ACTION:
through the looking glass

In the video this week, Jon talks about the looking glass theory. According to this theory, we become who the most important person in our life thinks we are. This week, you are invited to explore the implications of this theory.

Grab four index cards (or a sheet of paper which you can divide into four separate pieces). Now, take a moment to pray and think about who the three most influential people in your life are (or have been). Write each of their names on a card.

When you are done, take each card (one at a time), turn it over, and write down what this person taught you about love — good or bad — by how he or she lived. No one will see this list except you.

Take the final index card and write down the name of someone to whom *you* are important. Again, this is not someone who matters to you as much as it is someone with whom you know you have influence. This can be a child, spouse, girlfriend or boyfriend, coworker, or friend. Once you have written down the name, flip the card over and briefly note what you are teaching that person about love through your actions. Be thoughtful and prayerful about this process.

Finally, on the same side of the index card, write down one thing you can do this week to "show" that person what God's love looks like. It could be a note of encouragement, an act of kindness, or just a resolve not to roll your eyes once when he or she annoys you. Be creative! Once you have your idea, put affection into action and do it! Make notes about what you did so you can share how it went with the group during the next session.

Pray. Act. God is near.

AFFECTION IN DEVOTION: from the bowels?

For this week's "Affection in Devotion," read this potent and powerful passage from 1 John 3:16–18:

> 16This is how we know what love is: Jesus Christ laid down his life for us. And we ought to lay down our lives

for our brothers and sisters. [17]If anyone has material possessions and sees a brother or sister in need but has no pity on them, how can the love of God be in that person? [18]Dear children, let us not love with words or speech but with actions and in truth.

The letters of John (of which there are three) were texts written to mature Christians. As opposed to some of the other letters in the New Testament that addressed the challenges and mistakes of younger churches (think 1 Corinthians or Galatians), 1 John was meant to instruct Jesus followers who had been in the faith awhile. This is the kind of "solid food" teaching, not "milk," that Paul refers to in 1 Corinthians 3:2. What is at the heart of it is the very nature of love.

The apostle John is challenging us to make love more than a feeling. Love is not just affection or sentiment; it is about action and truth. This implies an agreement between the interior and exterior life (does this sound familiar yet?). Critical here is the way John links love's outward expression with generosity and compassion. He asks how the love of God can be in us if we see people in need and do not help them. This is indeed an important question for us today.

So, what does this look like? How do we do this? Perhaps verse 17 as rendered in the King James Version can help: "But whoso hath this world's good, and seeth his brother have need, and shutteth up his bowels of compassion from him, how dwelleth the love of God in him?" The *bowels* of compassion? This sounds silly to contemporary ears, but it is actually a great rendering of this text because it gets at the heart of what John is trying to address: a person's inner life. The Greek word used is *splagnon*, and it means our guts, our bowels, that innermost part of us. It is something that can be open or closed to those around us.

Do you know what this place is in you? What is the switch that opens you to compassion, mercy, and grace? John says that God's love flips on that switch *to everybody*. The question is: Do we want that?

We close our *splagnon* when we've been hurt, or we are tired, or we are just feeling selfish. That's why John reminds us that we don't have to try to muster up compassion when it's not there. We can trust God's love to open it for us. We just have to be willing to receive God's love first. Are you *open* to that?

- On a scale of 1 to 10, with 1 being totally closed and 10 being wide open, how open are you to God's love in your life right now? _____

- What are the circumstances in your life that affect how you answered that question?

- Where is one place in your life that you could act with more generosity as a way of demonstrating your openness to God's love? Share it with the group next week.

AFFECTION IN INSTRUCTION: rest

Read chapter 7 of the book *Jesus Prom*, and then reflect on the following questions.

- When do you rest?

- What does rest look like when you do it?

- Jon says, "Rest is a verb that is intentionally void of action. Rest requires inaction." What are ways to rest that are inactive? Are there ways to rest that are active?

- What would bad inaction and good inaction look like in your life?

- What is one way you can choose to rest this week?

- What is one "sometime" activity that you can make a "today" activity this week?

Use the space below to write any key points or questions you want to bring to the next group meeting.

SESSION THREE

see

see (v.) — to become aware
of something or someone by
using your eyes

introduction

In his book *Outliers*, Malcolm Gladwell famously asserts that it takes ten thousand hours of practice to become an expert at something. This means that mastering anything from playing a cello to swinging a golf club involves long hours of dedication. Expertise does not happen by accident. It happens on purpose.

Take a moment to think about the experts you most admire in your life, whether they are mentors, friends, or even celebrities. The way these people became excellent in their craft was by saying yes to some things and no to others. One does not become a virtuoso piano player without practice—that is what the player says yes to. However, in the process of saying yes to that rehearsal and training, the person must also say no to goofing off, pursuing other interests, and even extra free time. The discipline involved with this process—knowing what to say no to so you can know what to say yes to—comes into focus when we know what we want most.

The question to ask ourselves this week is: What do we want the most? What is the compass that drives our yeses and noes? Is it God? Do we want what God wants? If we do, how do we get there? The first answer to this question is that we trust God with *all* of ourselves. We entrust God with our desires and ask him to bend them into his own desires. This is not easy to do, and sometimes we can't see the way forward. But that's okay. Each of us walks by faith, not by sight.

checking in

Go around the group and answer the following question:

> When people think about habits, most often they
> imagine *bad* behaviors that are hard to kick. What
> would be a *great* habit to have?

Last week, you were invited to act in the "Between-Sessions Personal Study and Reflection" section. Discuss the following:

- Did you do at least one of the activities? If so, which one? If not, why not?

- What are some of the things you wrote down in reflection?

- What did you learn by engaging in these activities?

- What did you learn about yourself this week? About God?

hearing the word

Read John 11:1–7, 17–44 aloud in the group, listening for a fresh insight during the reading. Then together discuss the questions that follow.

> ¹Now a man named Lazarus was sick. He was from Bethany, the village of Mary and her sister Martha. ²(This Mary, whose brother Lazarus now lay sick, was the same one who poured perfume on the Lord and wiped his feet with her hair.) ³So the sisters sent word to Jesus, "Lord, the one you love is sick."
>
> ⁴When he heard this, Jesus said, "This sickness will not end in death. No, it is for God's glory so that God's Son may be glorified through it." ⁵Now Jesus loved Martha and her sister and Lazarus. ⁶So when he heard that Lazarus was sick, he stayed where he was two more days, ⁷and then he said to his disciples, "Let us go back to Judea."…
>
> ¹⁷On his arrival, Jesus found that Lazarus had already been in the tomb for four days. ¹⁸Now Bethany was less than two miles from Jerusalem, ¹⁹and many Jews had come to Martha and Mary to comfort them in the loss of their brother. ²⁰When Martha heard that Jesus was coming, she went out to meet him, but Mary stayed at home.
>
> ²¹"Lord," Martha said to Jesus, "if you had been here, my brother would not have died. ²²But I know that even now God will give you whatever you ask."
>
> ²³Jesus said to her, "Your brother will rise again."
>
> ²⁴Martha answered, "I know he will rise again in the resurrection at the last day."
>
> ²⁵Jesus said to her, "I am the resurrection and the life. The one who believes in me will live, even though

they die; 26and whoever lives by believing in me will never die. Do you believe this?"

27"Yes, Lord," she replied, "I believe that you are the Messiah, the Son of God, who is to come into the world."

28After she had said this, she went back and called her sister Mary aside. "The Teacher is here," she said, "and is asking for you." 29When Mary heard this, she got up quickly and went to him. 30Now Jesus had not yet entered the village, but was still at the place where Martha had met him. 31When the Jews who had been with Mary in the house, comforting her, noticed how quickly she got up and went out, they followed her, supposing she was going to the tomb to mourn there.

32When Mary reached the place where Jesus was and saw him, she fell at his feet and said, "Lord, if you had been here, my brother would not have died."

33When Jesus saw her weeping, and the Jews who had come along with her also weeping, he was deeply moved in spirit and troubled. 34"Where have you laid him?" he asked.

"Come and see, Lord," they replied.

35Jesus wept.

36Then the Jews said, "See how he loved him!"

37But some of them said, "Could not he who opened the eyes of the blind man have kept this man from dying?"

38Jesus, once more deeply moved, came to the tomb. It was a cave with a stone laid across the entrance. 39"Take away the stone," he said.

"But, Lord," said Martha, the sister of the dead man, "by this time there is a bad odor, for he has been there four days."

40Then Jesus said, "Did I not tell you that if you believe, you will see the glory of God?"

⁴¹So they took away the stone. Then Jesus looked up and said, "Father, I thank you that you have heard me. ⁴²I knew that you always hear me, but I said this for the benefit of the people standing here, that they may believe that you sent me."

⁴³When he had said this, Jesus called in a loud voice, "Lazarus, come out!" ⁴⁴The dead man came out, his hands and feet wrapped with strips of linen, and a cloth around his face.

Jesus said to them, "Take off the grave clothes and let him go."

What is one detail that stuck out to you from this story?

The mourners responded in one of two ways when they saw Jesus weeping. Some said, "See how he loved him!" (v. 36), while others said, "Could not he who opened the eyes of the blind man have kept this man from dying?" (v. 37). Which response do you relate to more?

watch the video

Watch the session 3 video clip, using the space below to take notes. When the video ends, take a moment to reflect and jot down one or two things you learned, disagreed with, or were surprised by.

group discussion

1. Jon says that "death blurs our vision." What does this phrase mean to you?

2. Describe a time in your life when you were able to live "by faith and not by sight."

3. What things in your life are easy to entrust to Jesus? What areas are hard to entrust to him? Why is it easy to trust God with some things and not others?

4. Why is Bill's story a story of redemption?

5. Would Bill's story still be an inspiring one if he didn't become a pastor? Why or why not?

6. Jon closes the video by saying, "Someday, you'll see Jesus. But you need to know … you can't unwrap your own grave clothes. You won't crawl out of the casket by your own power. You'll need help." What does this mean to you? How do we help "unwrap each other's grave clothes?" What does this look like, practically?

being the church

This session, we have been talking about trusting God with our lives. Some things are easy to entrust to God; some things are more difficult.

For this exercise, start with everyone in the sitting position (on a chair, a stool, a pew, whatever). Now stand up and look at where you have been sitting. You put the full force of your body weight on those pieces of furniture because you trusted them. You believed they would support and hold you up; you trusted them not to let you fall. This exercise is about learning to trust God the same way.

With everyone still standing, close your eyes and recall that area of your life that is difficult to entrust to God — whether it's your finances, your children, or your future, etc. Once you have settled on something, take a deep breath and, as a way of demonstrating your trust in (or your desire to trust in) God, sit back down. This week, use your faith in your seat as a symbol of how you can have faith in God for whatever your need.

closing prayer

After everyone is seated, silently take as much time as you need to pray and contemplate where you and God go next. While you are praying, breathe deep the peace of God.

between-sessions
PERSONAL STUDY AND REFLECTION

AFFECTION IN ACTION: **lists in the graveyard**

In this session of *Jesus Prom*, Jon emphasizes living "by faith and not by sight," even when it comes to our own death. Death gets us thinking about life.

This week for "Affection in Action," you are invited to spend some time among the dead. Take a journal and pen and visit a graveyard, funeral, or even a hospital. While you are there (or after, if you're at a funeral), write down one or two honest questions that *you* have about death. Afterward, consider the following:

- How do these questions affect your life?

- What does God have to say in response to those questions?

Now, use the chart on the following page to make a start-doing and a stop-doing list. Put at least two things on each list.

Start Doing	Stop Doing

Next, pick one item from each list to begin working on this week. If it's a start-doing item, consider what it will take to begin this new venture. What might you have to give up to make space for it? Who will it affect? How can others help you?

If it is a stop-doing item, consider why this habit is in your life in the first place. Is it covering up something else or substituting itself to meet a need that should be met another way?

Finally, consider what you want more. If it is just you pitted against your own desires, you'll fail every time. God wants to capture your imagination with something better—the stick instead of the walnut, to use Jon's metaphor from the video.

Make a few notes about your experience to share with the group next week.

Sit. Breathe. Trust. God is near.

AFFECTION IN DEVOTION: faith not sight

For this week's "Affection in Devotion," read this passage from Paul in 2 Corinthians 5:5–10:

> [5]Now the one who has fashioned us for this very purpose is God, who has given us the Spirit as a deposit, guaranteeing what is to come.
> [6]Therefore we are always confident and know that as long as we are at home in the body we are away from the Lord. [7]For we live by faith, not by sight. [8]We are confident, I say, and would prefer to be away from the body and at home with the Lord. [9]So we make it our goal to please him, whether we are at home in the body or away from it. [10]For we must all appear before the judgment seat of Christ, so that each of us may receive what is due us for the things done while in the body, whether good or bad.

In this passage, Paul is making an appeal to the Corinthian community to see their present lives in light of their future ones. It is important to note here that the future life Paul describes is not some "spiritual" existence but a physical one. The author is talking about resurrection!

For this reason, all the language about "the body" has a double ring to it. It is a reference to both our physical bodies right now (the ones that will pass away before we receive our resurrection bodies) and the habits of our old lives. So, when Paul talks about being "at home in the body" as a state of being "away from the Lord," he is not saying that our bodies are bad things. What he is asking us to consider is if there are any sins we love more than we love God. Are there attitudes, behaviors, or opinions from our old life—the one we lived before we met Jesus—that we need to give up?

If so, it's okay. We just need to recognize those things and lay them down, recognizing that what God promises to us in Christ is far superior to anything our bad habits can offer. It may not look like it at the time, but we can trust that it is so. This is because, as Paul says, sometimes we have to live by faith and not by sight.

But what about the language concerning judgment that comes at the end of the passage? The judgment seat of Christ is a reminder of two things. The first is the accountability we have to God for the life he has given us. Every person on earth will have to stand before God and say, "Here is what I made of the life you gave me."

However, the second thing the judgment seat reminds us of is that God has promised to make everything right. Remember, in the Bible the judgment of God is primarily a positive thing (see Psalm 98). It is something we need, not dread. Jesus knows our flaws and accepts us, warts and all.

- Where do you most need to live by faith and not by sight?

- What do your eyes "see" that is tempting to you?

- What does being "at home in the body" mean in your life?

- Is there anything in your heart that needs to be put to death because it is killing you? If so, what is it? How will you put it to death?

AFFECTION IN INSTRUCTION: die

Read chapter 5 of the book *Jesus Prom*, and then reflect on the following questions.

- In this chapter, Jon says, "When we die to self, we give life to others." What does that mean to you?

- Jon sets an alarm on his phone to remind him of God's love and that he should love others. How do you think your day would change if you adopted this same practice? (Consider doing this at least one day this week!)

- Reread the story of Marc in this chapter and think of a person in your life who has treated you badly. Is it possible he or she had some other need that drove the behavior? If so, what could that be?

Consider for a moment whether that person is not your enemy but someone in need. Pray on this for a moment. Now hold that person up in prayer and ask God to meet whatever need he or she has. Close by using the space below to write any key points or questions you want to bring to the next group meeting.

dance

dance (v.) — to move with the music

introduction

How do you feel about dancing? Is it something you like to do a lot? Or just at special events like weddings? When was the last time you really cut a rug and let it all hang out? If you're like most of us, the answer is probably "a long time ago."

Dancing, by its very nature, can be wild and unpredictable. When we dance, we have to be spontaneous, flexible, and creative. But we have to be something else as well: willing to look foolish … and that requires risk. Putting ourselves out there requires us to trust those around us with the areas in which we look silly, goofy, or just uncoordinated. It also requires that we trust ourselves—and God— enough to let go.

The problem is that most of us tend to arrange our lives to *reduce* risk. We want our lives to be safer. The pursuit of what our culture deems successful, our fears of the unknown, and our experience of loss all cultivate in us a desire for the predictable, protected, and secure. This is not altogether bad, but taken too far it can put us in a place where we are trapped … in our own security.

Our ability to take risks and trust in God moves against our internal "security prisons." That is what this week's session is all about. Jon has titled the entire book *Jesus Prom* because this kind of go-for-broke dancing is what God wants to do with all of us. In fact, it's Jon's metaphor for the great big party that is the kingdom of God. When we give ourselves over to this dance, we are saved from the shackles of safety and are released to love others, and ourselves, like God does. We get to have lives of true joy.

With an introduction like this, you might be a little nervous about what lies ahead of you in this session. You're not wrong. This session is going to ask a little more of you than the others have so far, but that is because it is important to give God space to get behind your walls of protection, fear, and security. This does not mean you're going to have to share your deepest, darkest secrets or anything like that. But it does mean that you are going to get invited to dance. The invitation of *Jesus Prom* is to be open for what God has for you this week and trust that wherever he leads you—even if it's onto the dance floor— will indeed be the way of life.

checking in

Go around the group and complete the following sentence:

One of the best presents I ever received was a

_____.

Last week, you were invited to act in the "Between-Sessions Personal Study and Reflection" section. Discuss the following:

• Did you do at least one of the activities? If so, which one? If not, why not?

• What are some of the things you wrote down in reflection?

- What did you learn by engaging in these activities?

- What did you learn about yourself this week? About God?

hearing the word

Read Acts 3:1–10 aloud in the group, listening for a fresh insight during the reading. Then together discuss the questions that follow.

> [1]One day Peter and John were going up to the temple at the time of prayer — at three in the afternoon. [2]Now a man who was lame from birth was being carried to the temple gate called Beautiful, where he was put every day to beg from those going into the temple courts. [3]When he saw Peter and John about to enter, he asked them for money. [4]Peter looked straight at him, as did John. Then Peter said, "Look at us!" [5]So the man gave them his attention, expecting to get something from them.
>
> [6]Then Peter said, "Silver or gold I do not have, but what I do have I give you. In the name of Jesus Christ of Nazareth, walk." [7]Taking him by the right hand, he helped him up, and instantly the man's feet and ankles became strong. [8]He jumped to his feet and began to walk. Then he went with them into the temple courts, walking and jumping, and praising God. [9]When all the people saw him walking and praising God, [10]they recognized him as the same man who used to sit begging at the temple gate called Beautiful, and they were filled with wonder and amazement at what had happened to him.

- Which character in the story do you relate to most (Peter and John, the lame man, all the people)? Why?

- What is one thing Christians today can learn from this story?

watch the video

Watch the session 4 video clip, using the space below to take notes. When the video ends, take a moment to reflect and jot down one or two things you learned, disagreed with, or were surprised by.

group discussion

1. Jon notes how people respond physically to love (e.g., Donnie hugs Jon; Peter takes the lame man's hand; the lame man dances). Does love always evoke a physical response? Why or why not?

2. Jon says, "The reason religious people feel threatened by joy is because they can't control it. Religious people love control, but joy can't be contained or confined or corralled." Who are these "religious people"? Do you think this statement about them is true? Why or why not?

3. What did you think of the way Brewster described the Jesus Prom? Would you want to go? Why or why not?

4. Think about the way Brewster sees the world. Which aspect of this do you most want for yourself?

5. Complete this sentence: "My life is so much better with _____ in it." For Jon, this is the handicapped and disabled. Who is it for you, and why?

6. Do you like to dance? Why or why not? (This may seem like a silly question, but it will come into play below.)

being the church

For this activity, you will need something that will work as a limbo stick (such as a broom pole or PVC pipe), some limbo (or other) music, and a music player. You may also want to have snacks, drinks, party hats, and streamers. (NOTE: If some members of your group have physical limitations, or if your space will not allow for the party exercise, you can substitute another party game such as charades, pin the tail on the donkey, or Simon Says.)

———

During this session, Jon emphasizes two important things. First, love evokes a *physical* response. It calls us to act.

Second, the kingdom of God is like a party. In fact, many of the metaphors Jesus used to talk about the kingdom of God involved a party. Given this, if our call is to bring heaven to earth, we need to practice God-blessed partying. This is precisely what the group is going to do now — by limbo dancing!

This will feel awkward, and maybe even a little threatening, but it's supposed to. The purpose of the exercise is to shake everyone out of their comfort zone, complacency, and cynicism so we can join the party of God.

Begin by setting up the limbo stick and starting the music. For the remainder of the study time, dance, laugh, and enjoy yourselves!

Once everyone has partied a bit, regroup and explore the following:

- What was this experience like for you?

- Did you find it difficult or easy? Why?

- What did you learn?

- How is a spontaneous party like the Jesus Prom that Jon talked about?

- Where could you throw other parties like this in your life?

closing prayer

Close by praying together this popular rendition
of the prayer that Jesus taught his disciples to pray
in Matthew 6:9-13:

> Our Father, who art in heaven,
> Hallowed be thy Name,
> Thy kingdom come,
> Thy will be done,
> On earth as it is in heaven.
> Give us this day our daily bread.
> And forgive us our trespasses,
> As we forgive those who trespass against us.
> And lead us not into temptation,
> But deliver us from evil.
> For thine is the kingdom, and the power,
>   and the glory,
> For ever and ever. Amen.

between-sessions

PERSONAL STUDY AND REFLECTION

AFFECTION IN ACTION: throw a party

For Jon's church, the Jesus Prom is their way of living
Jesus' instruction to throw a party for the people on the
margins of society — for those who cannot pay you back.

Now it's your turn.

This week, you are invited to plan and execute a party
for someone who is not expecting it or cannot pay you
back. You only have a week, so the party doesn't have
to be elaborate or fancy. It could be as simple as inviting
a single parent over for dinner, taking someone who is
lonely out to lunch, or even buying a gift for someone just
because they might like it. You could also bring a music
player to work and invite your coworkers to limbo with
you! The point is to stretch your brain and get creative.
Say a prayer about who in the regular orbit of your life
might need a party, and then scheme how you might
throw one to bless them.

After you throw your party, reflect on what it was like to
take on this audacious caper. What did you learn about
the coming kingdom (which is also like a party)? How
was the party you threw something that helped all the
participants train for the party of the new heaven and

new earth? Make notes so you can share how it went with the group during the next session.

Dance. Serve. Be the kingdom of God.

AFFECTION IN DEVOTION:
parable of the wedding banquet

For this week's "Affection in Devotion," read this passage from Luke 14:1, 7–24, which is one of Jesus' prominent teachings about the kingdom of God. You might even call it the "party of God" based on the reading, but this party doesn't work like other parties.

> [1]One Sabbath, when Jesus went to eat in the house of a prominent Pharisee, he was being carefully watched ...
> [7]When he noticed how the guests picked the places of honor at the table, he told them this parable: [8]"When someone invites you to a wedding feast, do not take the place of honor, for a person more distinguished than you may have been invited. [9]If so, the host who invited both of you will come and say

to you, 'Give this person your seat.' Then, humiliated, you will have to take the least important place. [10]But when you are invited, take the lowest place, so that when your host comes, he will say to you, 'Friend, move up to a better place.' Then you will be honored in the presence of all the other guests. [11]For all those who exalt themselves will be humbled, and those who humble themselves will be exalted."

[12]Then Jesus said to his host, "When you give a luncheon or dinner, do not invite your friends, your brothers or sisters, your relatives, or your rich neighbors; if you do, they may invite you back and so you will be repaid. [13]But when you give a banquet, invite the poor, the crippled, the lame, the blind, [14]and you will be blessed. Although they cannot repay you, you will be repaid at the resurrection of the righteous."

[15]When one of those at the table with him heard this, he said to Jesus, "Blessed is the one who will eat at the feast in the kingdom of God."

[16]Jesus replied: "A certain man was preparing a great banquet and invited many guests. [17]At the time of the banquet he sent his servant to tell those who had been invited, 'Come, for everything is now ready.'

[18]"But they all alike began to make excuses. The first said, 'I have just bought a field, and I must go and see it. Please excuse me.'

[19]"Another said, 'I have just bought five yoke of oxen, and I'm on my way to try them out. Please excuse me.'

[20]"Still another said, 'I just got married, so I can't come.'

[21]"The servant came back and reported this to his master. Then the owner of the house became angry and ordered his servant, 'Go out quickly into the streets and alleys of the town and bring in the poor, the crippled, the blind and the lame.'

²²"'Sir,' the servant said, 'what you ordered has been done, but there is still room.'

²³"Then the master told his servant, 'Go out to the roads and country lanes and compel them to come in, so that my house will be full. ²⁴I tell you, not one of those who were invited will get a taste of my banquet.'"

Notice that the whole affair began with Jesus eating dinner at the home of a well-known religious leader. Everyone at the table was jockeying for position, because in that time where you sat at the table denoted how important you were. That, in turn, denoted your value as a person.

This all seems unfair and unusual to our modern ears, but it did not seem strange to Jesus' contemporaries at all. This was how the societal game worked. You threw parties as a way of building social capital for yourself, and you used the table as a way to bring others into your debt. It was just how things were done.

All this is what made Jesus' challenge in verses 8–11 so revolutionary. Jesus told the guests to quit vying for first place and start vying for *last* place. Then he told the host that the next time he threw a party, he should not invite anyone who could bring him any gain; he should only invite people who could never pay him back. *"What?"* the host might say. *"That makes no sense. That would defeat the whole point of throwing a dinner party in the first place."*

Exactly. And that's the point.

Jesus had an entirely different take on why we throw parties. The question for us today is whether we see our parties more like Jesus does or more like the Pharisee and his friends did. Then, based on how we see them, what will we do next?

- What do you think was Jesus' reason for throwing parties?

- In the parable above, the crippled, the blind, and the lame were brought into the party. Who are these people in today's society?

- What would it mean to throw a party for them and invite them in?

- What are two concrete ways you could be part of throwing them such a party?

AFFECTION IN INSTRUCTION: dance

Read chapter 9 of the book *Jesus Prom*, and then reflect on the following questions.

- Jon says, "The quality of your life is tied to the quality of the love you give to others. God has placed a lot of people around you who need to be exposed to a higher quality of love." To whom does this apply in your life? Write down that person's name. How are you being called to demonstrate a higher quality of love to him or her?

- Who has loved you enough to help you across the finish lines in your life? Write down their names here, thank God for them, and then take a few minutes to send them an email, text, or social media message just to say thanks.

- How does the name *Jesus Prom* capture the theme of this whole book?

Use the space below to write any key points or questions you want to bring to the next group meeting.

give

give (v.)—to freely transfer
possession of

introduction

As a woman named Nicky was coming home from work, a young man approached her, asking for public transit fare. He seemed to be about her age, race, and socioeconomic class, but as she talked to him, their exchange took an interesting turn.

> Him: "Can you help me? I got robbed of my iPhone and wallet, and now I can't get back to the city on the train. Could you please buy me a ticket?"

> Nicky: "Sure, I'll help you."

> Him: "I'm not a bum, I promise."

> Nicky: "That's a weird thing to say."

> Him: "No, I just mean, I have a job."

> Nicky: "Then you're lucky. I'm helping you because you need help, not because you're 'not a bum.'"

> Him: "Yeah, but you know what I mean. I'm a graphic designer."

> Nicky: "Do you want to keep explaining about how you're better than other people, or do you need my help right now?"

After this exchange, he got silent, she bought him the train pass, and they parted ways.

This is a true story, and as it turns out, the guy was indeed a scam artist working the area. This makes his approach to soliciting money, however, all the more telling. He assumes that people will only give to someone in need if they think the person is "deserving." His insistence that he "had a job" and "was not a bum" is based on his reading of what people in our culture value and what they do not.

All of this makes Nicky's response even more perfect. Nicky is a Christian, and because of this, she has a different set of values about giving. She knows that God gives, not out of merit, but because he loves. She knows that the kingdom of God is a place where no one "gets what they deserve," but instead everyone gets what they need. She also knows that giving, in this context, sometimes involves saying no as much as it can require saying yes, and that she is the steward of wealth that is not her own. Her job is to get God's resources to where God wants them to go.

What would you have done if you were Nicky? These complicated dynamics of giving are exactly what you are invited to explore in *Jesus Prom* this week. *Why* do we give as Christians? *How* should we give? And, moreover, what does it mean to give in the manner that God does?

checking in

Go around the group and answer the following question:

> What is a charity, movement, or individual that you
> have supported financially? (This can be anything from
> a child sponsorship to dropping a dollar in the plate
> at church.)

Last week you were invited to act in the "Between-
Sessions Personal Study and Reflection" section. Discuss
the following:

- Did you do at least one of the activities? If so, which
  one? If not, why not?

- What are some of the things you wrote down in
  reflection?

- What did you learn by engaging in these experiments?

- What did you learn about yourself this week?
  About God?

hearing the word

Read Acts 5:1–10 aloud in the group, listening for a fresh insight during the reading. Then together discuss the questions that follow.

[1]Now a man named Ananias, together with his wife Sapphira, also sold a piece of property. [2]With his wife's full knowledge he kept back part of the money for himself, but brought the rest and put it at the apostles' feet.

[3]Then Peter said, "Ananias, how is it that Satan has so filled your heart that you have lied to the Holy Spirit and have kept for yourself some of the money you received for the land? [4]Didn't it belong to you before it was sold? And after it was sold, wasn't the money at your disposal? What made you think of doing such a thing? You have not lied just to human beings but to God."

[5]When Ananias heard this, he fell down and died. And great fear seized all who heard what had happened. [6]Then some young men came forward, wrapped up his body, and carried him out and buried him.

[7]About three hours later his wife came in, not knowing what had happened. [8]Peter asked her, "Tell me, is this the price you and Ananias got for the land?"

"Yes," she said, "that is the price."

[9]Peter said to her, "How could you conspire to test the Spirit of the Lord? Listen! The feet of the men who buried your husband are at the door, and they will carry you out also."

[10]At that moment she fell down at his feet and died. Then the young men came in and, finding her dead, carried her out and buried her beside her husband.

- What was wrong with what both Ananias and Sapphira did?

- What is something the church today can learn from this story?

watch the video

Watch the session 5 video clip, using the space below to take notes. When the video ends, take a moment to reflect and jot down one or two things you learned, disagreed with, or were surprised by.

group discussion

1. At the beginning of the video, several stories are shared about creative generosity (leaving big tips at restaurants, giving away your car, etc.). How did those stories make you feel? Were you more inspired or intimidated?

2. Jon says in the video, "Generosity isn't measured by how much you give away but by how much you keep for yourself." Do you think this is true? Why or why not?

3. In Stephen's testimony, he talks about being "blessed." What does that word mean to you? How does the Bible use it?

4. How is Stephen's life and perspective an example of Jesus-centered generosity?

5. What is the connection between generosity and joy? Have you ever experienced this? If so, describe.

6. Jon suggests, "Money is the source of most idolatry today." What does his comment mean to you? Do you think he's right?

being the church

Jon sent his church out to demonstrate what the incarnation was "really about" by acting with radical generosity. In a nutshell, because God gave his best to us in Jesus, we in turn should give our best to each other. When it comes to giving, however, many folks want to help but feel like they are not sure where to start. How much is too much to give? What if I don't give enough? What if I don't have enough to give enough? Here's where the words of John the Baptist are helpful.

When the crowd asked him how to prepare for the coming of the Messiah and the kingdom of God, he instructed them to share what they had: "Anyone who has two shirts should share with the one who has none, and anyone who has food should do the same" (Luke 3:11). It seems that our hearts are prepared for God through sharing, and this week, we are going to see if Jon was right.

Consider all of your possessions (don't exclude the things that are dearest to you!). Do you own more than one of something? Use the space below to make a list. These can be big or small items; brainstorm until you come up with at least three ideas.

This week, choose one of these "sets" and give the best of the two items away. This can be a direct gift to someone in need, or you can sell the item in question and donate the money. If both items are too beat up to give away, consider following Jon's lead and buy a new item to give away. Whatever you choose, remember to perform this activity as an expression of prayer and worship. Trust that God will use your gift to provide for the needy and open your heart more fully to his kingdom generosity.

After everyone has had time to make their list, go around the room and explore the following questions:

- Does anyone want to share what he or she is considering giving away? How does this make you feel?

- Does anyone need help narrowing down their list or deciding the recipient of their gift?

- How does this exercise make you feel on a scale from "inspired" to "intimidated"?

closing prayer

Close with a prayer resolving to complete this act of planned generosity and asking God to use this exercise for his glory this week.

between-sessions

PERSONAL STUDY AND REFLECTION

AFFECTION IN ACTION: give it away

For your "Affection in Action" time this week, you are invited to complete the planned generosity you conceived of at the end of session 5's group gathering. If you missed the video discussion, that's okay. Just read this week's "Being the Church" section (above), and follow the directions on finding something to give away.

The point of this week's exercise is to practice giving our best, not our leftovers. Make sure to jot down a few notes about your experience to share next time.

BONUS EXERCISE:

If you have already completed the "If you have two, give one" exercise, or want a deeper challenge, find a place to be extravagantly generous this week. Leave a huge tip for a meal or your morning coffee. Buy dinner for a stranger or even give someone in need a bicycle. You know what you have. Now release your control, and, like our God does, just give it away freely. (If money is tight right now, consider giving extravagantly with your time, attention, or service. Feel free to be as creative as you are generous, and make a few notes about your experience to share at the next session.)

AFFECTION IN DEVOTION:
loving those who don't love you back

For this week's "Affection in Devotion," begin by reading
Luke 6:27 – 38:

> [27]"But to you who are listening I say: Love your
> enemies, do good to those who hate you, [28]bless those
> who curse you, pray for those who mistreat you. [29]If
> someone slaps you on one cheek, turn to them the
> other also. If someone takes your coat, do not withhold
> your shirt from them. [30]Give to everyone who asks
> you, and if anyone takes what belongs to you, do not
> demand it back. [31]Do to others as you would have
> them do to you.
>
> [32]"If you love those who love you, what credit is that
> to you? Even sinners love those who love them. [33]And
> if you do good to those who are good to you, what
> credit is that to you? Even sinners do that. [34]And if
> you lend to those from whom you expect repayment,
> what credit is that to you? Even sinners lend to sinners,
> expecting to be repaid in full. [35]But love your enemies,
> do good to them, and lend to them without expecting
> to get anything back. Then your reward will be great,
> and you will be children of the Most High, because he
> is kind to the ungrateful and wicked. [36]Be merciful, just
> as your Father is merciful.
>
> [37]"Do not judge, and you will not be judged. Do not
> condemn, and you will not be condemned. Forgive,
> and you will be forgiven. [38]Give, and it will be given to
> you. A good measure, pressed down, shaken together
> and running over, will be poured into your lap. For with
> the measure you use, it will be measured to you."

Even folks unfamiliar with the Bible have heard the line, "Give and it will be given to you." Jon even mentions it in the video this week—and this portion of Luke's gospel is where it originates. What makes the context of this verse so interesting, however, is the way Jesus put a spin on what might feel like a familiar teaching.

The verse is embedded in Luke's account of the Sermon on the Mount. Jesus was in the middle of teaching what life looks like in the kingdom of God, and the conversation turned to how people treated their enemies. Jesus did not expect his followers *not* to have any enemies (following him faithfully would even create a few, he warned), but what he did expect was that his followers would deal with their enemies differently.

Instead of retaliating, taking revenge, or trying to destroy them, Jesus instructed his followers to hold their enemies up to blessing and prayer. Furthermore, Jesus said, the baseline for all human relationships is treating others as you would want to be treated. This means not just *not* taking revenge, but giving our money (or possessions)—without expecting reciprocation. Share, says Jesus, "without expecting to get anything back." "We're not playing a tit-for-tat game in regard to violence," he seemed to say, "so why would we play it with our checkbooks?" He is intent on drawing a distinction between the way of the world and the way of his kingdom, and that line seems to go right through the middle of our bank accounts.

So, don't judge others (or that will come back to bite you); don't condemn others (or you'll only end showing

how worthy you also are of condemnation); and give
without expecting repayment. God will make sure you
have everything you need. You can be openhanded.
Besides, the standard you use to treat others, concludes
Jesus, will be the way you get treated as well. Which begs
the question: What measure do you use? Is it Jesus', or
someone else's?

- Does this famous verse about giving (Luke 6:38) sound
  different to you in its context? If so, how? If not, why not?

- Why do you think Jesus makes a connection between
  money and violence?

- Is it realistic to actually lend to someone without
  expecting repayment? Why or why not?

- Is there an area of your life where you are playing the "tit-for-tat" game? What would it mean to have the volley stop with you?

AFFECTION IN INSTRUCTION: receive

Read chapter 14 of the book *Jesus Prom*, and then reflect on the following questions.

- Jon says, "I struggle to receive gifts … because of pride. I don't want to owe anyone anything." What is the connection between receiving and pride? Do you relate to Jon's statement? Why or why not?

- Would the people around you describe you as a generous person? Why or why not?

- Would the people around you describe your church as being a generous people? Why or why not?

- Jon closes the chapter with this line: "Grace doesn't exclude. Grace includes. It receives anyone who comes." What does this statement mean *to* you?

- What does this mean *for* you?

remember

remember (v.) — to keep an image in your mind

introduction

Welcome to the final session of your *Jesus Prom* experience. During this session, we will be visiting new content as well as reviewing previous material. If you have attended any of the past five weeks, you know our journey has been an exploration of words. This week's final session is no different. It is a call to *remember*.

Remembering has been central to the life of God's people from the very beginning. Throughout the Old and New Testaments, God called his followers to remember things: remembering what he had done or said, remembering what had happened during crucial periods in their history. Remembering is a key component to a vibrant life with God. However, another nuance to the word "remember" is also worth noting.

The word "remember" is made up of two smaller parts: the prefix *re*, which means "again," and *member*, which of course means something that is a part of a larger whole. Together they create the verb "remember," which involves connecting individual parts into a whole. Remembering is about putting scattered pieces back together.

This activity of gathering the scattered and bringing the isolated into community is what our God is all about. He even wants to put the broken pieces of his people back into place. That's why we are called to remember things. God uses our remembrances to bring us back into community, to remind us of our identity, and to give us a fresh vision for where we are going. Are you open to this?

Consider these ideas in the hour ahead, and be open to the way God might want to call you to remember. You can rely on the God of history to care for every part of you, and if any pieces are out of place, he would love to put them back where they belong.

checking in

Go around the group and answer the following question:

What was the last song you sang out loud?

Last week, you were invited to act in the "Between-Sessions Personal Study and Reflection" section. Discuss the following:

- Did you do at least one of the activities? If so, which one? If not, why not?

- What are some of the things you wrote down in reflection?

- What did you learn by engaging in these activities?

- What did you learn about yourself this week? About God?

hearing the word

Read Acts 16:16 – 34 aloud in the group, listening for a fresh insight during the reading. Then together discuss the questions that follow.

[16]Once when we were going to the place of prayer, we were met by a female slave who had a spirit by which she predicted the future. She earned a great deal of money for her owners by fortune-telling. [17]She followed Paul and the rest of us, shouting, "These men are servants of the Most High God, who are telling you the way to be saved." [18]She kept this up for many days. Finally Paul became so annoyed that he turned around and said to the spirit, "In the name of Jesus Christ I command you to come out of her!" At that moment the spirit left her.

[19]When her owners realized that their hope of making money was gone, they seized Paul and Silas and dragged them into the marketplace to face the authorities. [20]They brought them before the magistrates and said, "These men are Jews, and are throwing our city into an uproar [21]by advocating customs unlawful for us Romans to accept or practice."

[22]The crowd joined in the attack against Paul and Silas, and the magistrates ordered them to be stripped and beaten with rods. [23]After they had been severely flogged, they were thrown into prison, and the jailer was commanded to guard them carefully. [24]When he received these orders, he put them in the inner cell and fastened their feet in the stocks.

[25]About midnight Paul and Silas were praying and singing hymns to God, and the other prisoners were listening to them. [26]Suddenly there was such a violent earthquake that the foundations of the prison were

shaken. At once all the prison doors flew open, and everyone's chains came loose. [27]The jailer woke up, and when he saw the prison doors open, he drew his sword and was about to kill himself because he thought the prisoners had escaped. [28]But Paul shouted, "Don't harm yourself! We are all here!"

[29]The jailer called for lights, rushed in and fell trembling before Paul and Silas. [30]He then brought them out and asked, "Sirs, what must I do to be saved?"

[31]They replied, "Believe in the Lord Jesus, and you will be saved — you and your household." [32]Then they spoke the word of the Lord to him and to all the others in his house. [33]At that hour of the night the jailer took them and washed their wounds; then immediately he and all his household were baptized. [34]The jailer brought them into his house and set a meal before them; he was filled with joy because he had come to believe in God — he and his whole household.

- In verse 25, we read that Paul and Silas were singing while in prison. Why do you think they were singing? Would you be singing if you were in prison?

- What does this statement mean to you: "Believe in the Lord Jesus, and you will be saved — you and your household"?

- In the New Testament, "believing" in something meant to trust it. How does trusting Jesus rescue us?

watch the video

Watch the session 6 video clip, using the space below to take notes. When the video ends, take a moment to reflect and jot down one or two things you learned, disagreed with, or were surprised by.

group discussion

1. Jon talks about the word "joy" in this session. Is joy different from happiness? If so, how? If not, why not?

2. What does it mean to "focus on the cross while enduring hardship"?

3. How is Dewayne's story an example of Jon's statement that "Jesus died so you could live"?

4. What did Dewayne say he lost when he became a Christian? What did he gain?

5. What kinds of things does God ask us to remember today?

6. Jon says, "I want you to be able to rejoice in the Lord always! I want you to be able to say with confidence, 'I have learned to be content whatever the circumstance!'" Given this, is it okay for Christians to feel sad when tragedy befalls them? How does this relate to what Jon is saying?

7. How will you live today *remembering* that Jesus died so you could live?

being the church

For this activity, each of you will need one sheet of notebook paper, an envelope, and a pen. (You can also use printed thank-you cards if you prefer.)

———————

During this session, Jon notes that when Paul instructed the Philippian church to "rejoice always," it was not a suggestion. It was a command.

A command? Really?

How could Paul insist we rejoice? That seems counterintuitive to all the assumptions about emotion and spontaneity that we bring to the concept of rejoicing. But it is not. Rejoicing is something we can take on whenever we like. However, it *does* require training, and the way we train for rejoicing is through the practice of being grateful.

Gratitude makes it possible to be openhearted and thankful, even for the smallest things. Rehearsing the patterns of gratitude and cultivating them within ourselves may be countercultural, but it teaches us how to rejoice. Let's practice right now!

Using notebook paper and pen, write a thank-you note to someone in your life. This could be to anyone for anything — it just needs to be sincere and come from an authentic place in your heart. When you have completed your note, take an envelope that's been provided, put the note inside, and write the name of the recipient on the front.

When everyone has finished their notes, take a couple of minutes for those who would like to share who their note is to or what is about. Then take your note with you and resolve to mail it during the week. Use the following prompts to conclude your time together in *Jesus Prom*.

- As we conclude this study, one thing that changed in my thinking is _____ _____.

- The best thing about this experience was _____ _____.

- The worst thing was _____ _____.

- If I could describe my *Jesus Prom* experience in one word, it would be: _____.

closing prayer

Close the meeting by praying silently for the person on your left. Pray that he or she will have the courage to be a "noun" that loves the verbs Jesus loves, and one who will do the love of God wherever he leads.

in coming days

PERSONAL STUDY AND REFLECTION FOR THE COMING DAYS

AFFECTION IN ACTION: **from bad to good**

For this final "Affection in Action" section, you will need some modeling clay (Play-Doh® or the like).

In the video this week, Jon makes a profound point about the cross of Christ: it is God's way of showing that nothing is so bad that he can't make something good out of it. This statement of faith has been at the heart of the Christian witness for two thousand years, and this week you are invited to claim this truth for yourself.

Take the modeling clay and begin to knead it. While working it in your hands, consider something "bad" in your life that you would like (or need!) God to turn into "good." This can be a current circumstance, a painful memory, or just a feeling of regret. Whatever you choose, be honest about it.

When you've landed on your "bad," take a deep breath and form the clay into an object that represents that circumstance (abstract art counts!). As you do, remember the details of the event and consider what makes it a "bad" in your life. Once you have finished, set the object in front of you and observe it. Please note:

- Your object is NOT you. It is part of your life, but the object, like what it represents, is not the definition of your entire being.

- This object, like what it represents, is not bigger than God.

- This object, like everything else broken in this world, is something out of which God can bring something "good."

Now, when you are ready, take the object back into your hands. As an act of prayer and trust, refashion the object into the shape of a cross. Doing this will represent your way of saying yes to God's offer to bring "good" out of any "bad."

Once you have fashioned your cross, put it somewhere you will see it for the next couple of days. Let it serve as a reminder of God's goodness, power, and promise to heal everything. Also, start looking for what God might be doing with your "bad" already. He delights in healing broken things.

Pray. God is near.

AFFECTION IN DEVOTION: rejoice always!

For your final "Affection in Devotion," read the following excerpt from the apostle Paul's closing exhortations to the church at Philippi. He has said a great many things to them in this letter already, but as he moves toward his final point in Philippians 4:4–9, his words are powerful and pastoral.

> ⁴Rejoice in the Lord always. I will say it again: Rejoice! ⁵Let your gentleness be evident to all. The Lord is near. ⁶Do not be anxious about anything, but in every situation, by prayer and petition, with thanksgiving, present your requests to God. ⁷And the peace of God, which transcends all understanding, will guard your hearts and your minds in Christ Jesus.
> ⁸Finally, brothers and sisters, whatever is true, whatever is noble, whatever is right, whatever is pure, whatever is lovely, whatever is admirable—if anything is excellent or praiseworthy—think about such things. ⁹Whatever you have learned or received or heard from me, or seen in me—put it into practice. And the God of peace will be with you.

Notice that Paul begins by instructing this community to rejoice. As Jon pointed out in the video, rejoicing here is not a suggestion but a command. A command to rejoice? How were they supposed to do that? Was this just another form of legalism? As if to anticipate these very misgivings, Paul's follow-up sentence is, "Let your gentleness be evident to all. The Lord is near."

Huh? Gentleness? The Lord is near? What is Paul getting at?

In order to be gentle, you have to be able to relax. You have to be able to let go of your tension, anxiety, and fear. Gentleness comes with a confident realization that whatever you are trying to accomplish won't happen by force. Such gentleness flows from a posture of trust. When something (Someone) bigger than you is in control — when the Lord is near and active in your life — you can let go and relax. You're not so uptight about everything going wrong, because you don't have to run the show. You just have to do your part.

This is why gentleness and rejoicing both go with being a disciple of Jesus. Following Jesus is acknowledging that God is in control and we are not. It is settling into the restful reality that there is a center of the universe, and it's not us. It is opening our hands and releasing control only to find them full of life. From such a posture, rejoicing is easy. It is natural. Obvious. It's the most expected posture.

This is why Paul continues in verse 6 with an exhortation to not be anxious about anything. Why? Because we don't have to be. We can rejoice and know that the peace of God, which is bigger than our circumstances, will be with us always.

Rejoice, *be gentle*, *don't be anxious*, and *pray*. These are the verbs Paul invites the church to partake of in this passage of Scripture. How do these verbs sound to you?

- Which one of these verbs sounds like the best news to you?

• Which one is the hardest for you to do?

• Where in your life do you need "the peace of God which transcends all understanding"?

AFFECTION IN INSTRUCTION: verbatim and adverbs

Read chapters 15 and 16 of the book *Jesus Prom*, and then reflect on the following questions as you complete this study.

• Jon says, "Christians frequently visit Southland and say, 'I'm new to town and I'm church shopping. What do you all have to offer me?' Wouldn't it be great instead if people came to church and said, 'Here's what I can offer the church'?" Which of these postures best describes the way people see your church? Which one best describes the way *you* see your church?

- What does it mean for you to imitate Jesus? Which parts of your life are already Christlike, and which parts are not?

- What's the best verb you can use to help people see Jesus better today?

additional resources for group leaders

Thank you for giving of your time and talent to lead a *Jesus Prom* group study.

The *Jesus Prom* experience is a six-session study built around video content and small-group interaction. As group leader, imagine yourself as the host of a dinner party, whose job is to manage all the behind-the-scenes details so your guests can focus on each other and on interaction around the topic.

You need not answer all the questions or reteach the content — the video, book, and study guide do most of the work. Your job is simply to guide the experience and cultivate your small group into a learning community — a place for all of you to process, question, and reflect on what Jon Weece is teaching.

Make sure everyone in the group gets a copy of this study guide. Encourage them to write in their guide and bring it with them every week. This will keep everyone on the same page and help the process run more smoothly. Likewise, encourage every participant (or every couple) to get a copy of the *Jesus Prom* book so they can complete the "Affection in Instruction" reading assignments. Or see if anyone from the group is willing to donate an extra copy or two for sharing. Giving everyone access to all of the material will make this study the most rewarding.

hospitality

As group leader, create an environment as conducive to sharing and learning as possible. A church sanctuary or formal classroom may not be ideal for this kind of meeting because those venues can feel formal and less intimate. Wherever you choose, make sure there is enough comfortable seating for everyone, and, if possible, arrange the seats in a semicircle so everyone can see the video easily. This will make transition between the video and group conversation more efficient and natural.

Also, try to get to the meeting site early so you can greet participants as they arrive, especially newcomers. Simple refreshments create a welcoming atmosphere and can be a wonderful addition to a group study gathering. If you do serve food, try to take into account any food allergies or dietary restrictions group members may have. Also, if you meet in a home, find out if the house has pets (in case there are any allergies) and even consider offering childcare to couples with children who want to attend. Finally, be sure your media technology is working properly. Managing these details up front will make the rest of your group experience flow effectively and provide

a welcoming space in which to engage the content of
Jesus Prom.

leading your group

Once everyone has arrived, it is time to begin the group.
If you are new to leading small groups, what follows
are some simple tips to make your group time healthy,
enjoyable, and effective.

First, consider beginning the meeting with a word of
prayer, and remind people to silence and put away their
mobile phones. This is a way to say yes to being present
to each other and to God.

Next, invite someone to read the session's introduction
from this study guide to focus everyone on the week's
topic. After the "Checking In" time (see below), your
group will engage in a simple Bible study called "Hearing
the Word," drawn from the content of the video. You do
not need to be a biblical scholar to lead this effectively.
Your role is only to open up conversation by using the
instructions provided and to invite the group into the text.

Now that the group is fully engaged, it is time to watch
the video (the videos range from 15–20 minutes,
depending on the session; space is provided in the study
guide for jotting notes). The content of each *Jesus Prom*
session is inspiring and challenging, so there is built-in
time for personal reflection before anyone is asked to
respond. Don't skip over this part. Internal processors
will need the more intimate space to sort through their

thoughts and questions, and it will make the group discussion time more fruitful.

During group discussion, encourage everyone to participate, but make sure that those who do not want to share know they do not have to (especially as the questions become more personal). As the discussion progresses, follow up with responses such as, "Tell me more about that" or, "Why did you answer the way you did?" This will allow participants to deepen their reflections and it invites meaningful sharing in a nonthreatening way.

Each session features multiple questions. You do not have to use them all or follow them in order. Pick and choose questions based on either the needs of your group or how the conversation is flowing. Also, don't be afraid of silence. Offering a question and allowing up to thirty seconds of silence gives people space to think about how they want to respond and also gives them time to do so.

As group leader, you are the boundary keeper for your group. Do not let anyone (yourself included) dominate discussion. Keep an eye out for group members who might be tempted to "attack" folks they disagree with or who try to "fix" those having struggles. Such behaviors can derail a group's momentum, so you need to discourage them. Model active listening and encourage everyone in your group to do the same. This will make your group time a safe space and foster the kind of community that God can use to change people.

As the discussion wraps up, the most dynamic part of the weekly study — "Being the Church" — begins. During this time, participants are invited to put what they have learned into practice. **Please read each "Being the Church" section prior to the meeting, as several of the activities require special materials.** Reading ahead will allow you to ask group members to bring any items you might need but don't have. It also will give you a sense of how to lead your group through the experience. Use the following supply list to make sure you have what you need for each session.

supply list

SESSION 1:
- pens (one per participant)
- index cards (one per participant)

SESSION 2:
- lined notebook paper (one sheet per participant)
- pens (one per participant)
- scissors (one per participant)
- glue sticks (one per participant)
- colored construction paper (one sheet per participant)

SESSION 3:
- a chair or place for every group member to sit (don't let anyone sit on the floor this week)

SESSION 4:
- limbo stick (broom pole, PVC pipe, etc.)
- music player

- CD or device with limbo music (or other music)
- snacks (optional)
- drinks (optional)
- party hats and streamers (optional)

SESSION 6:
- notebook paper (one sheet per participant)
- envelopes (one per participant)
- OPTION: use printed thank-you notes and envelopes instead
- pens (one per participant)

Finally, even though instructions are provided for how to conclude each session, feel free to strike out on your own. Just make sure you do something intentional to mark the end of the meeting. Also, take time before or after the closing prayer to encourage everyone to engage in the between-sessions personal study and reflection activities before the next gathering.

debriefing the between-sessions materials

As just noted, each session includes an on-your-own section where everyone is invited to choose one or more of the activities to complete. Your job is to help group members debrief these experiences during the next session's "Checking In."

Debriefing these activities is a bit different than responding to a video because the content comes from the participants' real lives. Though you are free to direct

this time as you like, the basic experiences that you want
the group to reflect on are as follows:

- What was the best thing about the activity?

- What was the hardest thing about it?

- What did you learn about yourself?

- What did you learn about God?

———————

Thank you again for taking the time to lead your group.
May God reward your efforts and dedication and make
your time together in *Jesus Prom* fruitful for his kingdom.

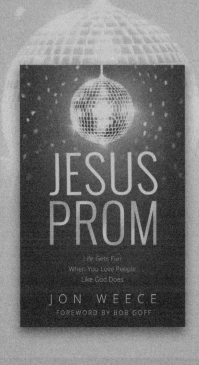

Wouldn't it make sense that if we claim we want to be like Jesus, we would want to do what he did? To *love* as he loved, *be* with others as he was with them, *see* with his eyes, *dance* with his joy, *give* like he gave, and *remember* like he remembered?

Nouns need verbs. That's more than just a grammatical truth—it's a spiritual truth. The noun *Christian* and the noun *church* require action verbs to fulfill their purpose. That's why Jesus invites Christians and churches everywhere to perform the greatest action of all: *loving people.*

Jesus Prom is an extravagant party that celebrates the very people Jesus died to love. You will laugh and cry as you move through the pages of this book, and by the end of it, you'll want to join the dance.

For videos, sample chapters, and all
***Jesus Prom* news, please visit JesusProm.com.**